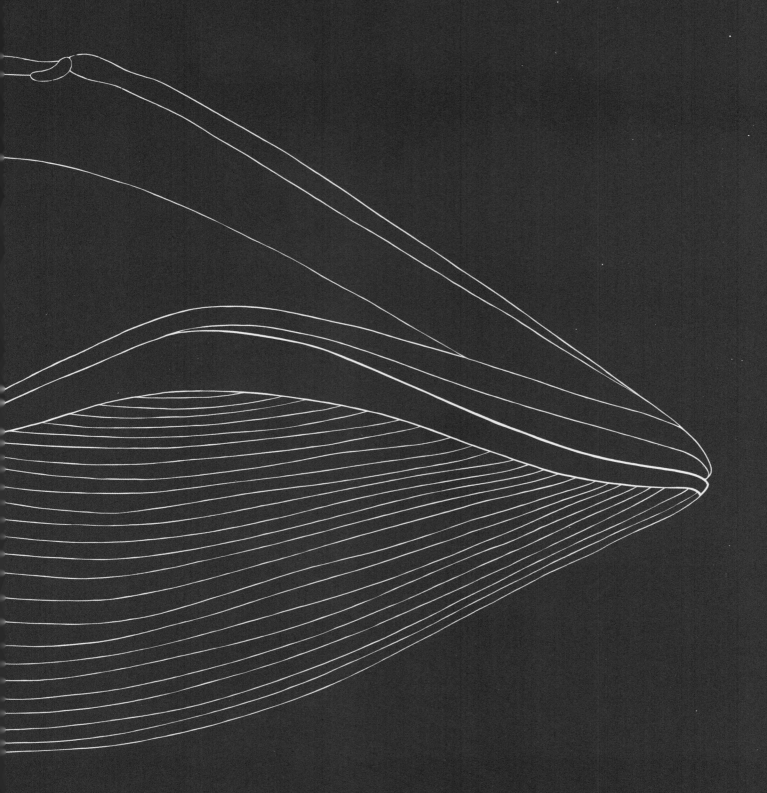

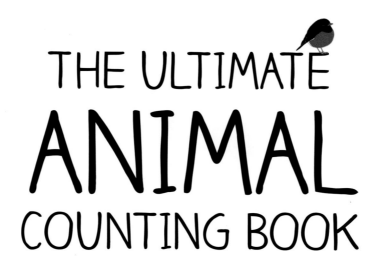

THE ULTIMATE
ANIMAL
COUNTING BOOK

Also by Jennifer Cossins

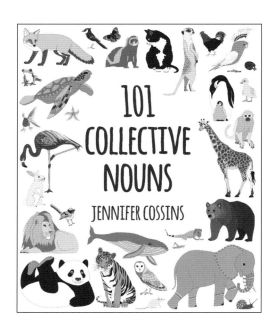

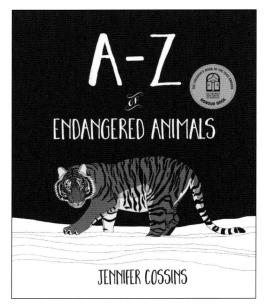

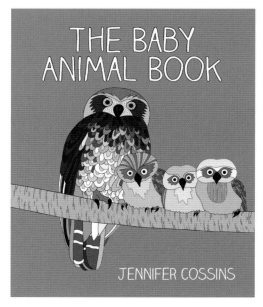

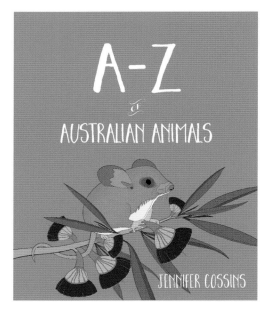

THE ULTIMATE
ANIMAL
COUNTING BOOK

JENNIFER COSSINS

LOTHIAN
Children's Books

A Lothian Children's Book

Published in Australia and New Zealand in 2019
by Hachette Australia
Level 17, 207 Kent Street, Sydney NSW 2000
www.hachettechildrens.com.au

5 7 9 10 8 6 4

A catalogue record for this
book is available from the
National Library of Australia

ISBN 978 0 7344 1885 2 (hardback)

Designed by Red Parka Press
Author photograph by Oliver Berlin
Colour reproduction by Splitting Image
Printed in China by Toppan Leefung Printing Limited

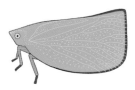

For my amazing, creative, animal-loving wife, Tracy.
My number one, forever and always.

xxx

The blue whale is the largest animal known to have ever lived, growing up to 30 metres long and weighing up to 180 000 kilograms.

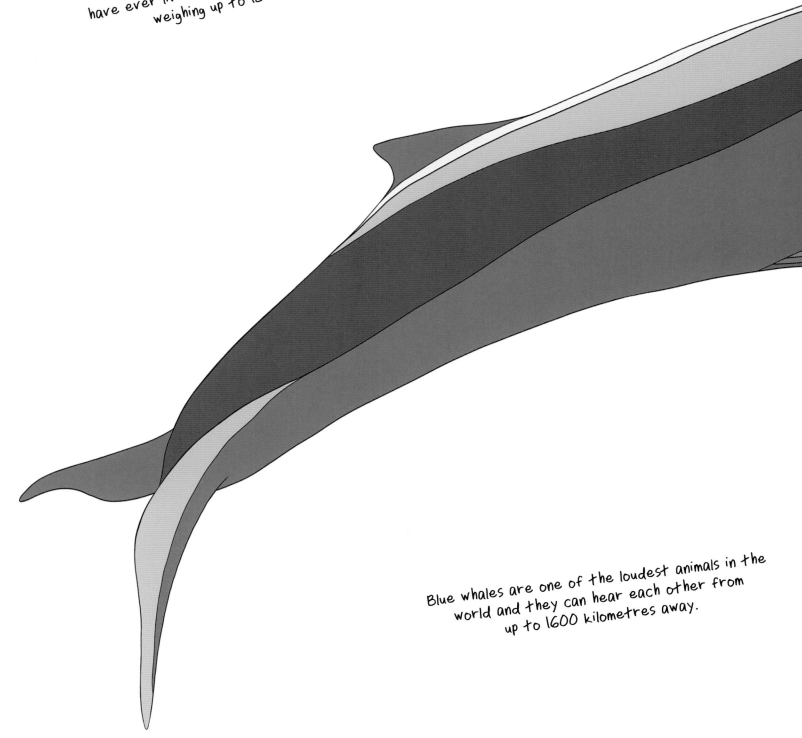

Blue whales are one of the loudest animals in the world and they can hear each other from up to 1600 kilometres away.

The tongue of a blue whale is huge and can weigh as much as an elephant.

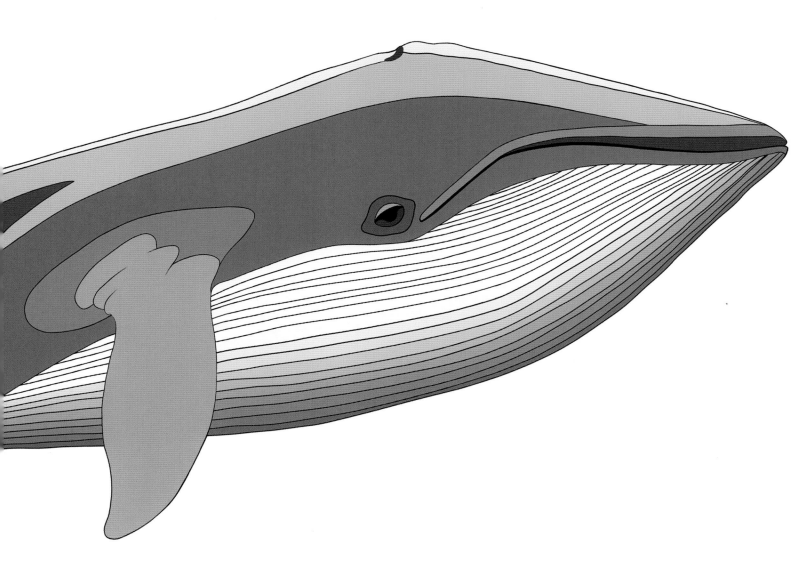

A blue whale's heart is as big as a car and it's loud – its beat can be detected from 3 kilometres away.

A baby blue whale weighs about 2700 kilograms at birth and drinks over 600 litres of milk a day.

2 Colossal Squids

Colossal squids live very deep in the ocean and are rarely seen, so not much is known about them.

The colossal squid is the largest squid in the world.

Colossal squids have light organs in their eyes that work like built-in headlights, helping them see in the deep, dark ocean.

Colossal squids have the largest eyes in the entire animal kingdom – they can be as big as a soccer ball.

Asian elephant

3 Elephants

Elephants are the largest land animals in the world, weighing up to 6000 kilograms.

Elephants are highly intelligent and empathetic animals.

African elephant

An elephant's trunk has over 40 000 muscles in it and is used to breathe, drink, gather food, smell, make noises and to pick things up.

Elephants can't jump.

4 Orcas

Orcas are also called killer whales but are actually a very large species of dolphin.

Orcas are around 8 metres long and weigh about 5500 kilograms.

Orcas are the greatest predators in the ocean, preying on anything they can find, including sharks, penguins, seals, fish, squid, sting rays and even whales.

Orcas are playful and curious creatures that live and hunt in groups called pods.

Much like different human cultures, each orca pod makes distinctive sounds and has its own food preferences.

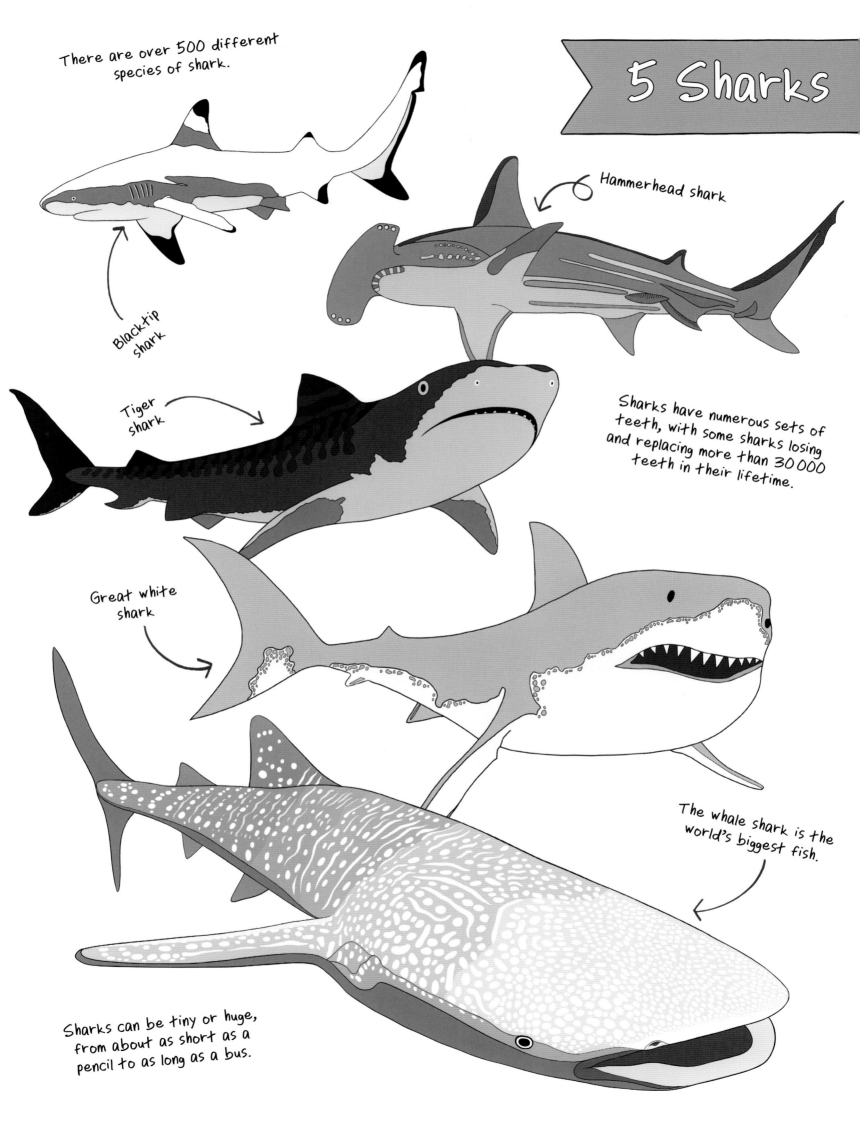

There are over 500 different species of shark.

5 Sharks

Hammerhead shark

Blacktip shark

Tiger shark

Sharks have numerous sets of teeth, with some sharks losing and replacing more than 30 000 teeth in their lifetime.

Great white shark

The whale shark is the world's biggest fish.

Sharks can be tiny or huge, from about as short as a pencil to as long as a bus.

6 Giraffes

Giraffes are the tallest living animals on earth at 4-5 metres tall.

South African giraffe

There are 9 recognised subspecies of giraffe. They live in different regions of Africa and have different patterns of markings.

West African giraffe

Reticulated giraffe

Giraffes give birth standing up, which means the baby falls about 2 metres to the ground.

A giraffe's tongue is around 50 centimetres long.

Every giraffe in the world has a unique pattern of spots.

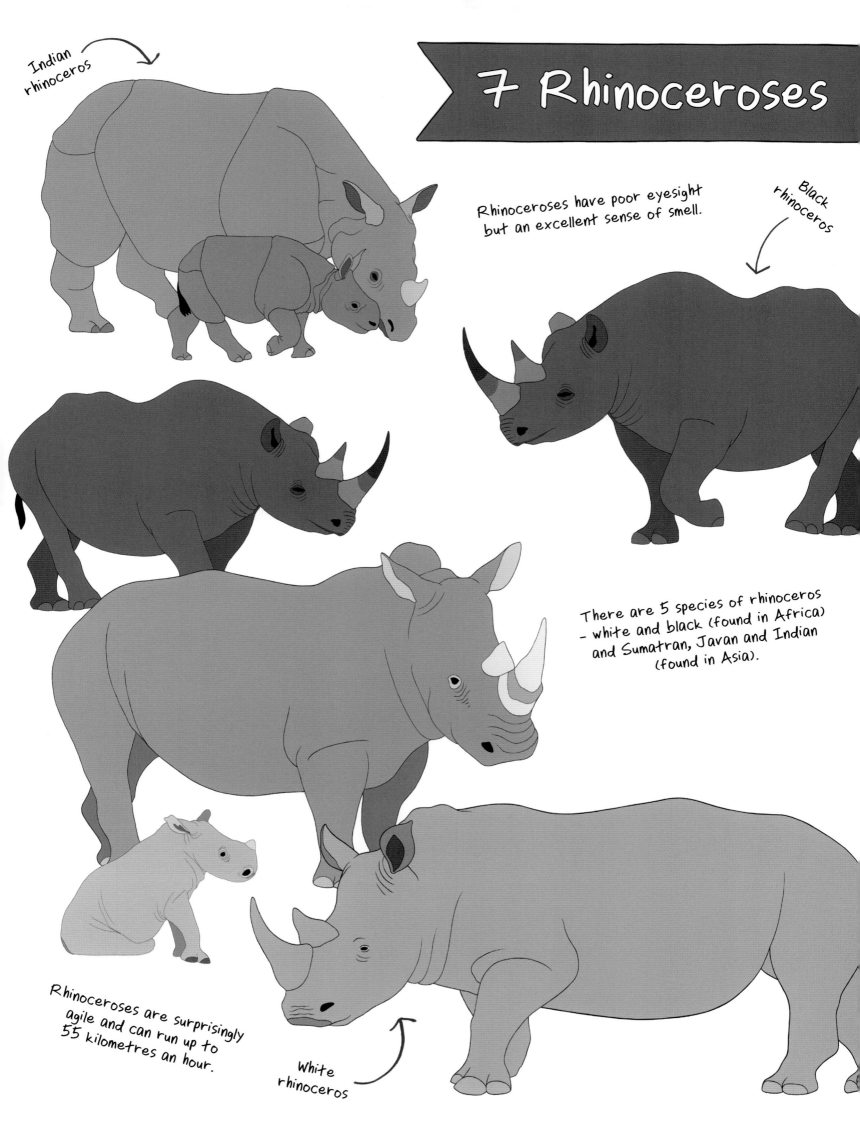

Indian rhinoceros

Rhinoceroses have poor eyesight but an excellent sense of smell.

Black rhinoceros

There are 5 species of rhinoceros - white and black (found in Africa) and Sumatran, Javan and Indian (found in Asia).

Rhinoceroses are surprisingly agile and can run up to 55 kilometres an hour.

White rhinoceros

8 Hippopotamuses

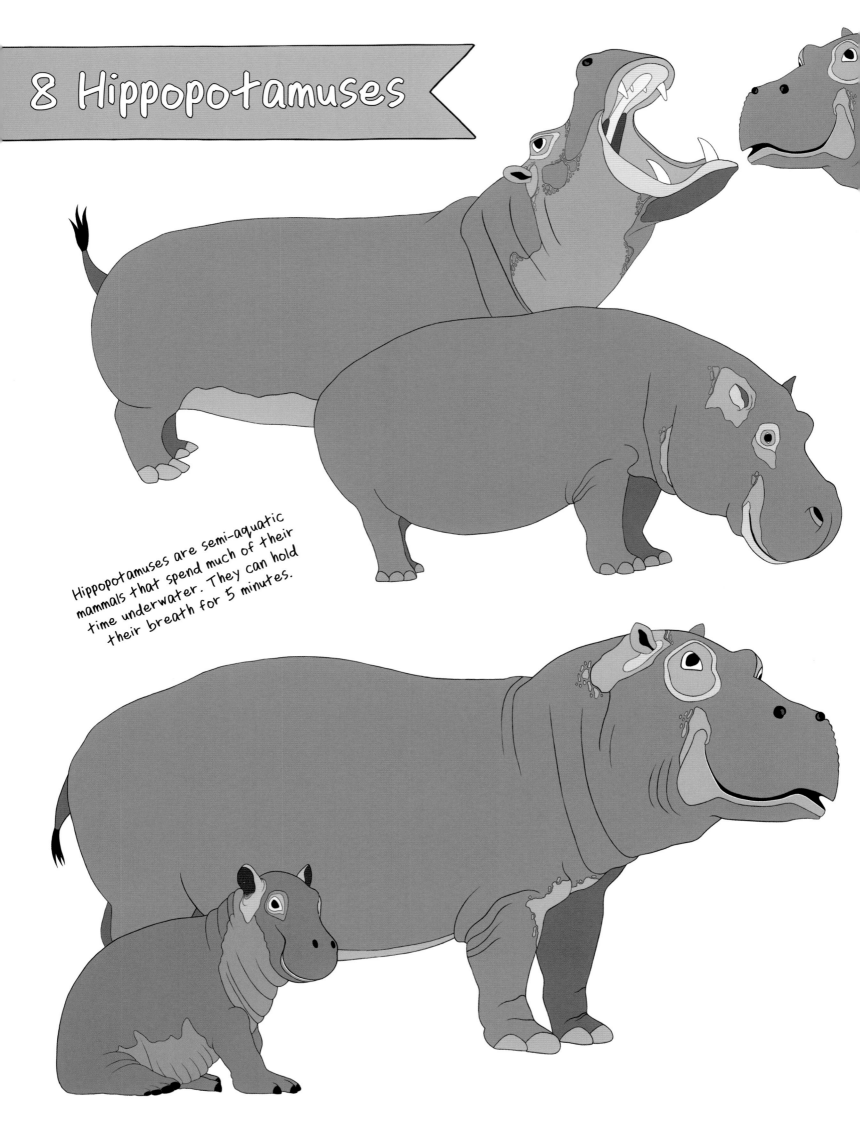

Hippopotamuses are semi-aquatic mammals that spend much of their time underwater. They can hold their breath for 5 minutes.

Hippopotamuses spend their days in the water, venturing on to land at night to graze.

The name 'hippopotamus' comes from ancient Greek and means 'river horse'.

Hippopotamuses have eyes, ears and nostrils high on their heads so they can see, hear and breathe while staying mostly underwater.

9 Tigers

Tigers are the largest wild cats in the world and can weigh over 300 kilograms.

Every tiger in the world has a unique pattern of stripes.

Tigers can run at around 65 kilometres an hour at full speed.

Unlike most cat species, tigers like swimming and often cool off in the water when it's hot.

Moose are the largest species in the deer family.

Moose are good swimmers and have nostrils they can close so they can graze underwater.

Moose hair is hollow to better insulate them from the cold.

Male moose lose their antlers once a year and grow new ones.

ll Polar Bears

Polar bears are marine mammals that spend most of their time on Arctic sea ice.

Polar bears have black skin under their fur.

Polar bears can be as long as 2.5 metres.

Polar bears look white but their hair is actually transparent. This reflects the light and helps them blend in on the ice.

A polar bear's sense of smell is so good it can sniff out its prey, usually seals, from up to I kilometre away.

Grizzly bears are also known as North American brown bears.

12 Grizzly Bears

Although grizzly bears are powerful hunters, they mostly eat berries, roots and nuts.

Grizzly bears are surprisingly fast for their size and can run up to 50 kilometres an hour.

Grizzly bears hibernate during winter.

13 Camels

Camels may look awkward but can run almost as fast as a horse.

Dromedary

There are 3 species of camel – the dromedary, which has one hump, and the Bactrian and wild Bactrian camel, which have two.

Camels live mostly in dry or desert regions. They have long eyelashes and special protective eyelids to protect their eyes from sand.

Bactrian camel

Camels can survive for much longer than other animals without drinking.

14 Highland Cows

Highland cows have the longest hair of any cow breed.

Highland cows originate from Scotland but are now found in many parts of the world.

The long hair that often covers a highland cow's eyes is called a dossan.

Highland cows have oiled hair that helps them stay dry in the rain.

15 Zebras

The mountain zebra is the smallest species of zebra.

A baby zebra is born with legs almost as long as an adult zebra.

Grevy's zebras are endangered and have rounder ears and more stripes.

Every zebra has a unique pattern of stripes.

Plains zebras are the most common species of zebra.

A zebra's skin is black under its white hair.

A group of zebras is called a dazzle.

All zebra species are native to Africa.

16 Lions

Lions like to relax, napping, resting or sleeping for up to 20 hours a day.

Lions can run at a speed of up to 81 kilometres an hour.

A group of lions is called a pride.

Lions are the only big cats that live in social groups.

A lion's roar is so loud it can be heard up to 8 kilometres away.

17 Wildebeest

Wildebeest are also called gnus.

Wildebeest are famous for their annual migration, where over a million wildebeest travel together across East Africa.

Wildebeest calves can walk within minutes of being born and, within a few days, can keep up with the herd.

18 Bongos

Bongos are large antelopes that live in Africa.

Bongos are mostly nocturnal animals.

Both male and female bongos have horns.

Bongos are timid creatures that are easily frightened.

Tapirs can be found in Central and South America as well as Asia.

Lowland tapir

Baby tapirs have stripes to help them camouflage.

Malayan tapir

Tapirs use their noses like snorkels when swimming.

A group of tapirs is called a candle.

20 Sea Turtles

Olive Ridley sea turtle

The gender of sea turtle babies is determined by the temperature of the nest where the eggs are laid, with hotter nests producing more females and cooler ones more males.

Sea turtles are ancient animals that existed back in the time of the dinosaurs.

Female sea turtles return to the same place every year to lay their eggs.

The leatherback sea turtle is the largest sea turtle, weighing up to 500 kilograms.

Green sea turtles can hold their breath underwater for 5 hours.

Sea turtles cry, but not because they are sad. They have a special gland that helps get rid of the salt in their eyes and this makes it look like they are crying.

21 Giant Pandas

Giant pandas are native to China.

Giant pandas live almost entirely on bamboo and have stomachs lined with mucus to protect them from bamboo splinters.

Unlike most bears, giant pandas do not hibernate.

At birth, baby giant pandas are about 15 centimetres long and blind, pink and hairless.

22 Horses

There are hundreds of different breeds of horse around the world.

The fastest horse ever recorded could run at 88 kilometres per hour.

A male horse is called a stallion and a female horse is called a mare. However, a young male is a colt and a young female a filly.

Horses can sleep lying down or standing up.

23 Jaguars

Jaguars are the third-largest big cat, after tigers and lions.

A jaguar's bite is the most powerful of all big cats.

Jaguars live in the Americas, mostly in dense rainforest.

Jaguars are an endangered species.

Jaguars are solitary creatures, only coming together with others to mate.

Jaguars stalk then ambush their prey, often leaping into the water or out of trees.

24 Emus

Emus are the second-tallest bird in the world after the ostrich - they can reach almost 2 metres tall.

The emu is Australia's largest native bird.

Emus are fast - they can run at about 50 kilometres an hour.

Female emus lay the eggs but it's the males that incubate them and then look after the chicks.

Okapis live in the African rainforests.

25 Okapis

Okapis have really long tongues – they can even lick their own ears.

Okapis are endangered and solitary creatures so it's very hard to see them in the wild.

Okapis are the only living relative of the giraffe.

26 Sea Lions

Sea lions are carnivores, eating mostly fish, squid and small octopus.

Sea lions are often mistaken for seals. Although they may look similar, they are quite different.

Sea lions are very social animals that like to huddle together to sleep and sunbathe on the beach.

Unlike seals, sea lions can lift their bodies off the sand and walk on their flippers.

A baby sea lion is called a pup.

Donkeys are highly social animals and seem to get very depressed if left on their own.

Donkeys have long memories and are very intelligent, with problem-solving skills comparable to dogs and dolphins.

Donkeys are very strong and are used as transport for people and goods in many countries.

The wild African donkey is critically endangered, with possibly as few as 50 left in the wild.

28 Wolves

The wolf is the largest member of the dog family.

Arctic wolf

A wolf pack is led by a mated pair – an alpha male and female. This pair is usually the only one that breeds while the rest of the pack help bring up the pups.

Wolves have small webs between their toes that make them good swimmers.

Wolves use various howls to communicate with each other.

Wolves are born with blue eyes that turn yellow, brown or grey when they are around 8 months old.

Despite its name, the grey wolf can be various shades of black, white or brown as well as grey.

29 Kangaroos

There are more kangaroos than people in Australia.

The red kangaroo is the world's largest marsupial, growing up to 2 metres tall.

Kangaroos can't move backwards.

A baby kangaroo is called a joey.

Joeys often dive head first into their mother's pouch when frightened.

Grey kangaroo

Kangaroos move their back legs together on land but when kangaroos swim they paddle one leg at a time, like a human.

Red kangaroos can jump 8 metres long and 3 metres high in one leap.

Sun bears are the world's smallest bear species.

They get their name from the golden patch on their chests.

Despite their name, sun bears are nocturnal.

Sun bears live in the tropical rainforests of Southeast Asia.

Sun bears have very long tongues that are good for getting honey out of bee nests.

31 Alpacas

A baby alpaca is called a cria.

Alpacas are members of the camel family.

Alpacas are friendly and curious animals, but they spit when they feel threatened.

Humming is the most common sound alpacas make.

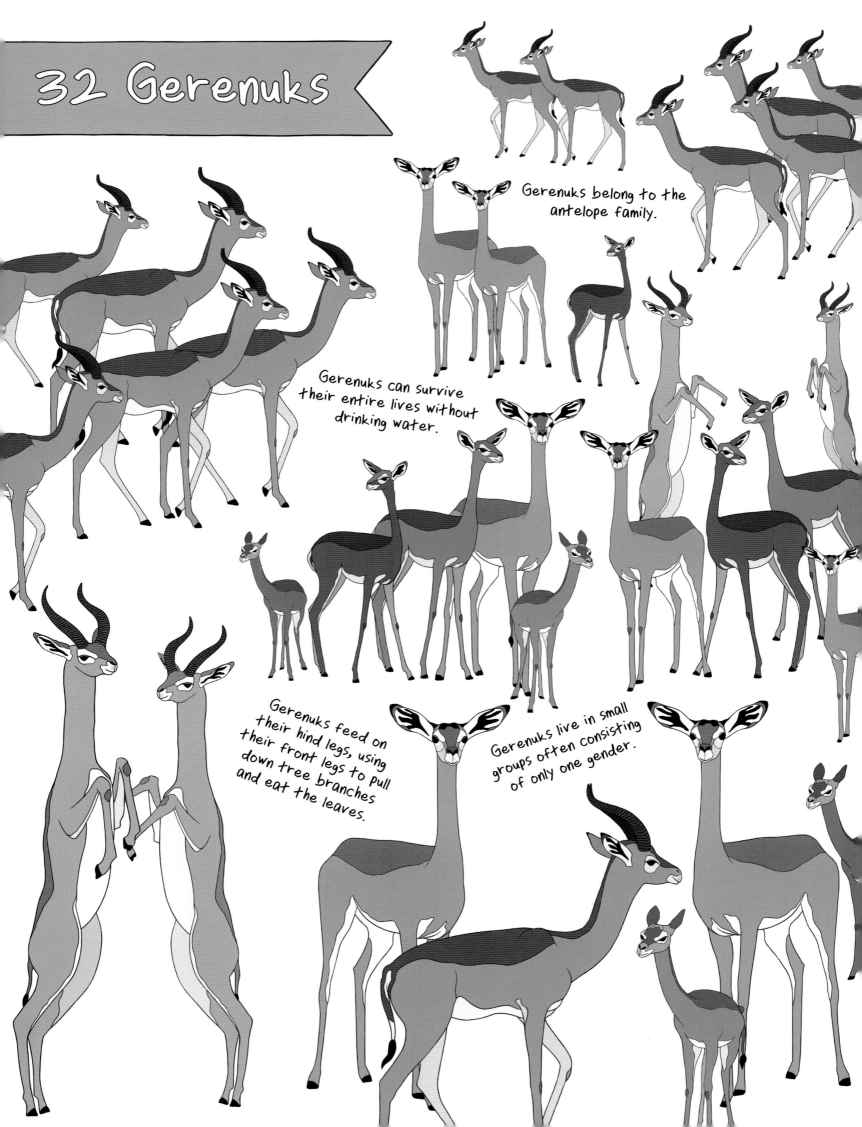

32 Gerenuks

Gerenuks belong to the antelope family.

Gerenuks can survive their entire lives without drinking water.

Gerenuks feed on their hind legs, using their front legs to pull down tree branches and eat the leaves.

Gerenuks live in small groups often consisting of only one gender.

There are over 200 breeds of goat.

Goats were one of the first animals to be tamed by humans.

Baby goats were called kids long before the word was used for human children.

Goats have rectangular pupils.

Goats have excellent balance and are good at climbing rocks, cliffs and trees.

Goats from different places have different accents that can change, joining humans, elephants, dolphins and bats as the 5 creatures known to change accent.

34 Flamingos

There are 6 different species of flamingo.

Chilean flamingo

Flamingos eat with their heads upside down.

American flamingo

Flamingo chicks are born with white feathers, black legs and straight beaks.

The greater flamingo is the tallest species, growing to 1.5 metres tall.

Spotted hyena

Spotted hyenas are sometimes called laughing hyenas because they sound like humans cackling.

There are 4 different species of hyena.

Spotted hyenas usually hunt for their food while striped hyenas are mostly scavengers.

Striped hyena

Hyenas are very intelligent with excellent problem-solving skills.

36 Pelicans

There are 7 different species of pelican.

Peruvian pelican

The Dalmatian pelican is the largest species of pelican.

Pelicans eat mostly fish, which they swallow whole.

American white pelican

American white pelican in flight

The brown pelican is the smallest species of pelican.

The Australian pelican has the longest bill of all bird species in the world.

Pelicans have a throat pouch under their bills called a gular that can hold 13 litres of water.

37 Cranes

The blue crane is one of the 6 species of crane that are endangered.

There are 15 different species of crane.

White-naped crane

Cranes are famous for performing elaborate and beautiful dances.

Sandhill crane

Most cranes mate for life.

Grey-crowned crane

38 Capybaras

Capybaras are native to South America.

Capybaras are the world's largest rodents.

Capybaras are very social animals and enjoy spending time with other species as well as other capybaras.

Capybaras can sleep in the water, with only their noses above the water to breathe.

Capybaras are good swimmers and like being in the water.

White-tailed eagle

There are over 60 different species of eagle.

Male and female eagles look similar but the females are much bigger.

Bald eagles are not really bald but named for the white feathers on their heads.

Eagles have excellent eyesight, powerful beaks and long talons, making them exceptional hunters.

White-bellied sea eagle

Eagles return to the same nest each year to lay their eggs.

The wedge-tailed eagle is the largest bird of prey in Australia and one of the largest eagles in the world.

40 Border Collies

Border collies are herding dogs that are often used on farms to herd sheep.

Border collies are one of the most intelligent dog breeds.

Border collies are most commonly black and white but can also be various shades of red, brown and gold.

Due to their intelligence, border collies make great search-and-rescue dogs.

Caracals are medium-sized wild cats that live in Africa and the Middle East.

Caracals are extremely fast – they can run up to 80 kilometres an hour.

Caracals are nocturnal animals.

Caracals are quite acrobatic and can leap 3 metres high to catch a bird in flight.

42 Wombats

There are 3 species of wombat and they are only found in Australia.

Common wombat

Wombat poo is cube-shaped.

Female wombats have backward-facing pouches so they can dig without dirt going inside.

The northern hairy-nosed wombat is endangered.

Wombats are the largest burrowing animals in the world.

Southern hairy-nosed wombats are smaller than northern ones and have slightly redder fur.

The fennec fox is the smallest fox in the world.

There are 12 different fox species.

Grey fox

Foxes are members of the dog family.

Foxes live all around the world in various climates, from the Arctic to the desert.

Red fox

A group of foxes is called a skulk.

There are 18 different species of penguin in the world and they all live in the Southern Hemisphere.

Adelie penguin

Only Adelie and emperor penguins live permanently in Antarctica. The other species live mostly in Australia, New Zealand and South America.

Little penguins are the world's smallest penguin, reaching about 35 centimetres tall.

Chinstrap penguin

Penguins can't breathe underwater but can dive for 10-20 minutes at a time.

Emperor penguins are the largest penguin and can be over 1 metre tall and weigh up to 40 kilograms.

45 Geese

Greylag goose

The red-breasted goose is an endangered species and lives mostly in Eastern Europe.

Unlike domestic geese, wild geese form monogamous pairs.

Most wild geese migrate up to 5000 kilometres every year, returning to the place they were born to lay their eggs.

Barnacle geese live in Northern Europe and the Arctic.

Canada goose

A female is called a goose while the male is called a gander.

Cape Barron geese live in the southern regions of Australia.

46 Sloths

There are 6 species of sloth.

Sloths are native to Central and South America.

Sloths are very slow moving animals that spend most of their time in trees.

Sloths only go to the toilet once a week.

Sloths can swim 3 times as fast as they can walk.

47 Beagles

Beagles are popular pets because they are very good natured and friendly.

Beagles are one of the most vocal breeds of dog.

Beagles can be trained to recognise over 50 different smells.

Because of their amazing sense of smell, beagles are often used by police or border security as sniffer dogs.

48 Ibises

There are 28 different species of ibis around the world.

Ibises are social birds that live in groups of hundreds or even thousands.

The Asian crested ibis is endangered.

Ibises have long curved bills that are used to help them find food in the mud.

American white ibis

Glossy ibis

Australian white ibis

The scarlet ibis gets its bright colour from eating crustaceans.

Coatis live in South and Central America as well as southern regions of North America.

Coatis can also be called coatimundis.

Male coatis are twice as big as females.

South American coati

Coatis are good tree climbers and their tails help them balance.

Coatis mostly move around with their tails up.

White-nosed coati

50 Owls

Owls live on all continents except for Antarctica.

Owls can turn their heads 270 degrees.

Barn owls eat over 1000 mice a year and swallow them whole.

There are over 200 species of owl in the world.

The southern boobook owl is the smallest and most common owl in Australia.

Snowy owls live in the Arctic regions of North America and Europe.

A group of owls is called a parliament.

51 Jackrabbits

Jackrabbits are a North American species of hare.

Jackrabbits can leap 3 metres in a single jump.

Jackrabbits are fast and hop in a zig-zag pattern to confuse predators.

Jackrabbits are good swimmers.

Jackrabbits will thump the ground with their back legs to warn others of danger.

The pink fairy armadillo is the smallest armadillo in the world at 13–15 centimetres long.

52 Armadillos

There are 21 species of armadillo.

All armadillos live in Central or South America except for the nine-banded armadillo, which also inhabits North America.

Six-banded armadillo

Armadillo means 'little armoured one' in Spanish.

Nine-banded armadillo

Armadillo armour is made of bone.

53 Pheasants

Pheasants were originally from Asia but can now be found all around the world.

The Mikado pheasant is native to Taiwan.

Some pheasant species can grow to almost 1 metre long, including their tail feathers.

Blood pheasants are named for the bright red colour on their breast, throat and forehead.

In China, the golden pheasant is a symbol of good luck and prosperity.

54 Red Pandas

Despite their name, red pandas are not pandas. They are sometimes called red bear-cats.

Red pandas live in the eastern Himalayas and south-western China.

Red pandas are endangered.

Red pandas use their tails to wrap around themselves to keep warm.

55 Toucans

Toucans live in the tropical forests of South America.

White-throated toucan

Choco toucan

Male and female toucans toss fruit to each other in mating rituals.

Keel-billed toucan

Channel-billed toucan

Toucans have a serrated bill to help tear their food apart.

Toco toucan

56 Macaws

Macaws mate for life.

Hyacinth macaws are the largest parrots in the world.

Blue-and-gold macaw

There are 17 species of macaw and many of them are endangered.

Red-and-green macaw

Scarlet macaw

Macaws are native to Central and South America.

Tasmanian pademelon

Pademelons are nocturnal.

Pademelons are small marsupials that live mostly in coastal regions of Australia.

Pademelons are macropods, meaning they belong to the kangaroo family.

Pademelons eat grass, leaves, moss, ferns and berries.

Red-legged pademelon

58 Gibbons

All gibbon species are endangered.

Gibbons spend most of their time in trees.

Yellow-cheeked gibbon females are mostly yellow but males are black with yellow cheeks.

Gibbons can swing between branches at great speed.

Agile gibbons are various shades of black and brown.

Gibbons are small apes with no tail and a human-like build.

The black Siamang gibbon is the largest and loudest of all gibbons.

Lar gibbons vary greatly in colour, from very light brown to black.

59 Chevrotains

Chevrotains are the smallest hoofed animal in the world.

Chevrotains vary in size from around 20-40 centimetres tall.

Chevrotains are also called mouse deers, though they are neither a mouse nor a deer.

Male chevrotains have tusk-like canine teeth used for fighting.

Chevrotains stomp their feet fast like a drumroll when agitated.

60 Lemurs

Black lemur males are black and females orange.

There are over 100 species of lemur.

Lemurs have two tongues.

Lemurs only live on Madagascar and a few other nearby islands.

Male lemurs get in stink-fights, where they rub their tails in their own scents and shake them at their opponents.

Red-ruffed lemur

Ring-tailed lemur

Unlike most mammals, in lemur society females are dominant over males.

61 Cats

There are over 50 breeds of domestic cat.

A group of cats is called a clowder but a group of kittens is called a kindle.

Adult cats don't meow at each other, only at humans.

It is thought cats were first domesticated over 4000 years ago.

On average, cats spend about two thirds of their time sleeping.

Cat eyes reflect light, giving them excellent night vision.

62 Ducks

Male ducks are called drakes, females are called hens and babies are called ducklings.

Ducks have a special blood-flow system to their feet that means their feet don't get cold.

Indian runner duck

Ducks often sleep in a row and the one at the end sleeps with one eye open to look out for danger.

The colourful Mandarin duck is native to East Asia.

Mallard ducks are the most common duck in the world.

There are 21 different species of cockatoo that live in Australia and parts of Southeast Asia.

Gang-gang cockatoo

63 Cockatoos

Cockatoos can live to 80 years old.

Sulphur-crested cockatoo

Yellow-tailed black cockatoo

Salmon-crested cockatoo

Female red-tailed black cockatoos have much more patterning than males.

Cockatoos are the loudest parrots in the world.

64 Chickens

Australorp chickens are a well-known breed from Australia and come in different colours.

Fear of chickens is called alektorophobia.

Silver-laced Wyandotte chicken

Chickens are intelligent birds that can recognise individual chickens within their social group.

There are an estimated 25 billion chickens in the world.

Male chickens are called roosters and female chickens are called hens.

Rhode Island red chicken

The chicken is the closest living relative to the Tyrannosaurus rex.

65 Oystercatchers

Oystercatchers form monogamous pairs.

Female oystercatchers are usually larger than males.

Oystercatchers are wading birds found in coastal regions around the world.

Their strong beaks are used to hammer or pry open shellfish, their favourite food.

Pied oystercatcher

The sooty oystercatcher is only found in Australia.

The kea is named after its loud, distinctive call.

The kea is a large parrot that is only found in New Zealand.

Keas are mostly olive green but have bright colours under their wings that are only seen when they fly.

The kea is the only alpine parrot in the world.

Keas are smart and curious birds with a reputation for damaging cars and stealing tourists' belongings.

67 Chihuahuas

Chihuahuas are on average around 20 centimetres tall.

The chihuahua is one of the smallest breeds of dog in the world.

Chihuahuas originally come from Mexico.

Chihuahuas tremble when stressed, excited or cold.

Chihuahuas can have long or short hair and many colour combinations.

Chihuahuas are too fragile to live outside, so must be indoor dogs.

Kiwis are flightless birds that are native to New Zealand.

Kiwis are the only bird in the world to have nostrils at the end of their beaks.

The kiwi is the national bird of New Zealand.

Kiwis are nocturnal.

Female kiwis lay huge eggs that can weigh up to a quarter of their weight.

Kiwis have whiskers.

69 Gulls

Gulls are often called seagulls but gull is the correct term.

There are around 50 species of gull in the world.

Gulls can unhinge their jaws to allow them to swallow large prey whole.

The silver gull is the most common gull seen in Australia.

Gulls are highly intelligent and inquisitive sea birds.

Unlike most animals, gulls can drink both fresh water and sea water.

The Pacific gull has the largest bill of all gull species.

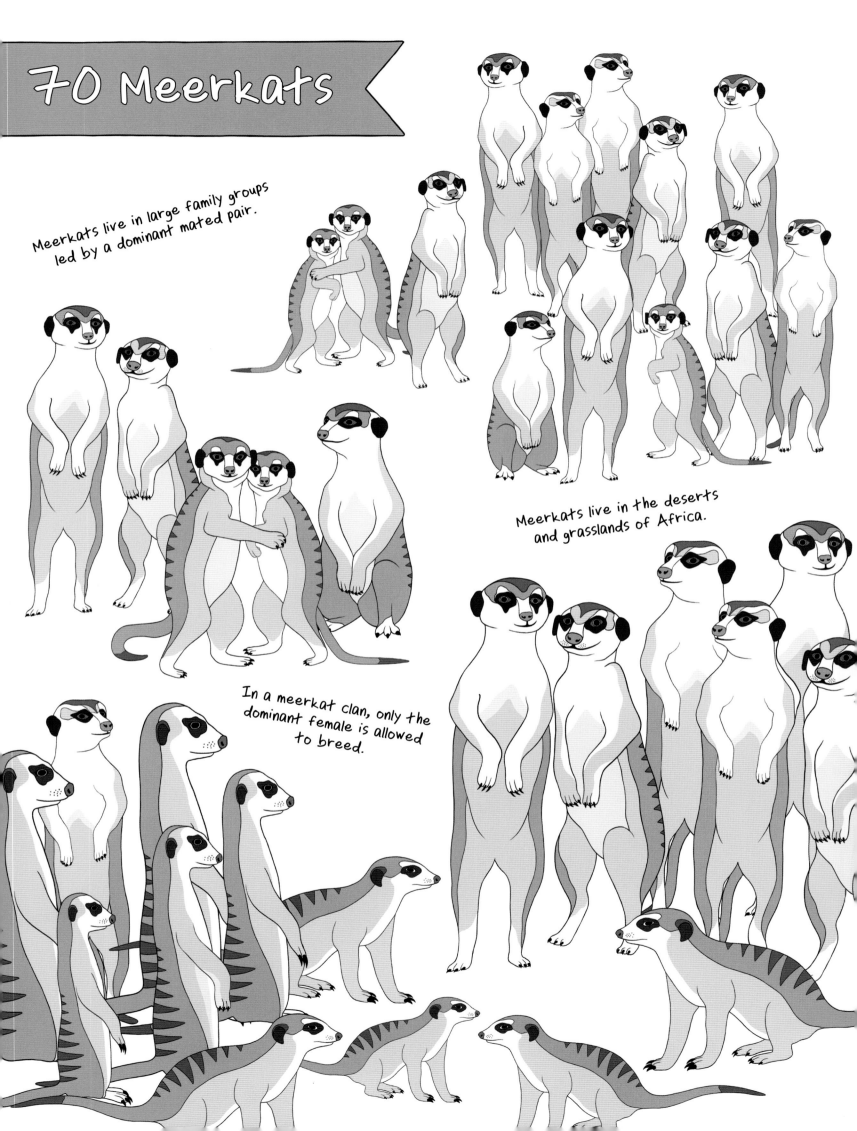

70 Meerkats

Meerkats live in large family groups led by a dominant mated pair.

Meerkats live in the deserts and grasslands of Africa.

In a meerkat clan, only the dominant female is allowed to breed.

If confronted by a predator, meerkats will stand up together, arch their backs and hiss.

Meerkats can recognise different meerkat voices.

When a family is relaxing, one meerkat will always stand tall, propped up by its tail, to look out for danger.

Meerkats groom each other to make friends.

71 Kookaburras

The kookaburra is the largest member of the kingfisher family of birds.

The laughing kookaburra is native to Australia.

Kookaburras are monogamous.

Blue-winged kookaburra males have blue tails as well as wings.

Kookaburras are famous for their laugh, which they use to mark their territory.

The Australian magpie is native to Australia and New Guinea.

Magpies are territorial and like to live in the same area for their whole lives.

Magpies are known for their beautiful, musical warbling.

A magpie's hearing is so good they can hear worms and bugs moving underground.

73 Sea Dragons

Sea dragons live in coastal waters among seaweed and kelp forests.

Sea dragons are only found in Australian waters.

Sea dragons are one of the most beautifully camouflaged creatures on earth.

Leafy sea dragon

Sea dragons don't have teeth or a stomach and suck their food in through their snouts.

Sea dragons are closely related to seahorses and pipefish.

Male sea dragons are responsible for incubating their mate's eggs on a spongy patch on their tails.

Weedy sea dragon

Sea dragons grow up to 35 centimetres long.

Golden-headed lion tamarin

Tamarins live in Central and South America.

Tamarins usually give birth to twins.

Emperor tamarin

The golden-headed lion tamarin is native to Brazil.

Tamarins are very small monkeys about 13-30 centimetres long, with tails often longer than their bodies.

A cotton-top tamarin's hair stands up when they're alarmed or excited.

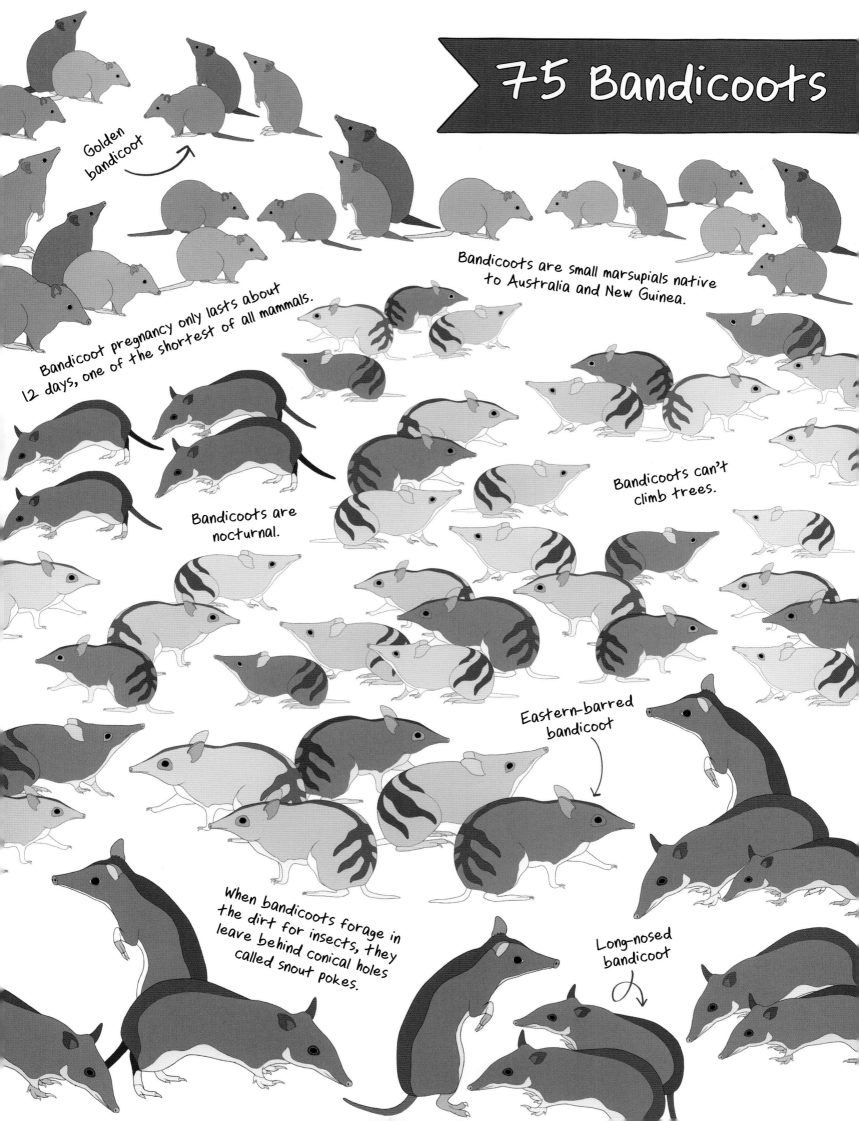

Golden bandicoot

Bandicoots are small marsupials native to Australia and New Guinea.

Bandicoot pregnancy only lasts about 12 days, one of the shortest of all mammals.

Bandicoots can't climb trees.

Bandicoots are nocturnal.

Eastern-barred bandicoot

When bandicoots forage in the dirt for insects, they leave behind conical holes called snout pokes.

Long-nosed bandicoot

76 Angelfish

The are many different angelfish species ranging in length from a few centimetres up to half a metre long.

Flame angelfish

The bright colours of angelfish look dramatic but they actually help them blend in with the colours and patterns of the reefs they inhabit.

Emperor angelfish

Regal angelfish

The peppermint angelfish is one of the rarest fish in the world, living extremely deep in the South Pacific Ocean.

Angelfish are born female. If the dominant male in a group dies or leaves, the dominant female will change into a male.

77 Flying Foxes

Flying foxes are often called fruit bats.

Flying foxes roost together in large groups of many thousands.

Black flying fox

Flying foxes mate upside down.

Little red flying fox

The grey-headed flying fox is the largest bat in Australia.

Spinifex pigeon

Male pigeons bow and coo to impress females in elaborate mating rituals.

Spinifex pigeons and crested pigeons are both native to Australia.

Crested pigeon

A baby pigeon is called a squab.

There are an estimated 400 million pigeons in the world.

Pigeons are highly intelligent and have amazing navigational skills.

Pigeons are monogamous.

Nicobar pigeon

There are about 55 different species of lorikeet.

Lorikeets are small parrots found in Australia and parts of Southeast Asia and Polynesia.

Musk lorikeet

Purple-crowned lorikeet

Lorikeets roost in large groups but during the day break into small groups or pairs.

Lorikeets have special brush-tipped tongues to help them eat nectar from flowers.

Lorikeets mate for life.

Lorikeets eat pollen, nectar, fruits and seeds.

Rainbow lorikeet

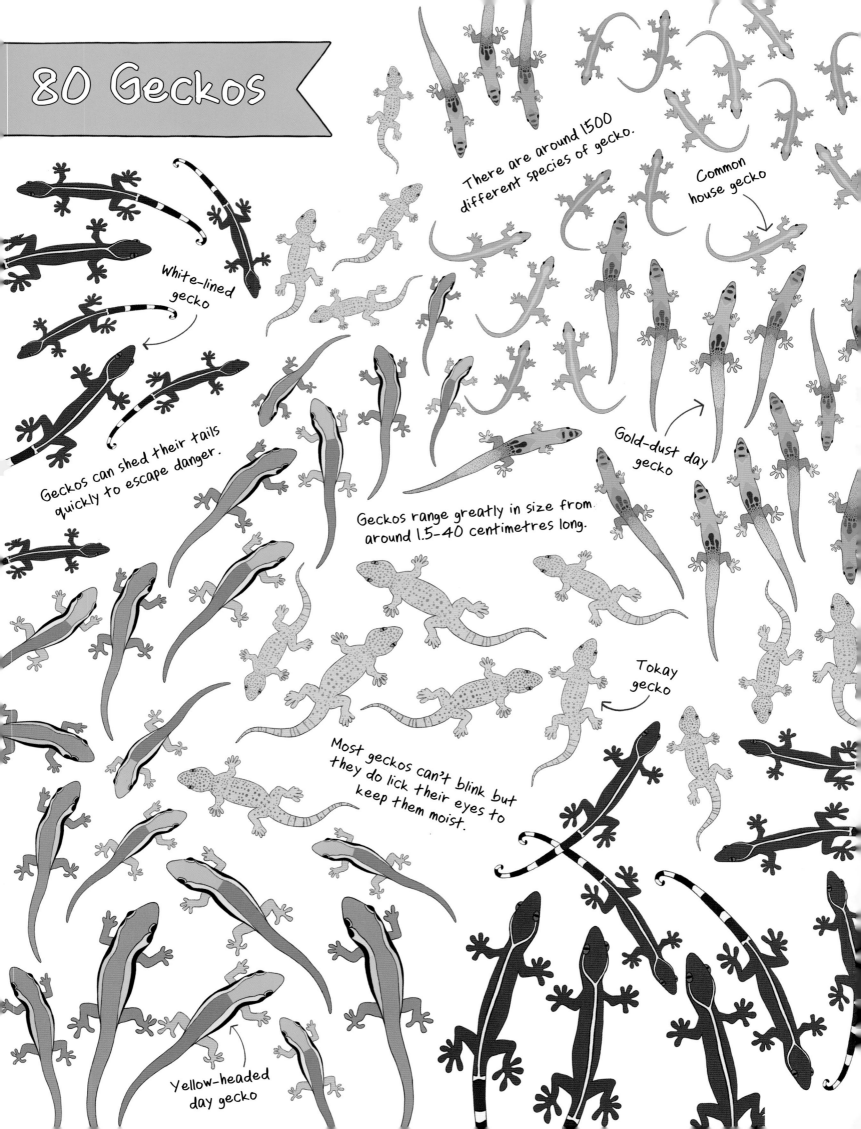

80 Geckos

There are around 1500 different species of gecko.

Common house gecko

White-lined gecko

Geckos can shed their tails quickly to escape danger.

Gold-dust day gecko

Geckos range greatly in size from around 1.5–40 centimetres long.

Most geckos can't blink but they do lick their eyes to keep them moist.

Tokay gecko

Yellow-headed day gecko

81 Honeyeaters

There are around 180 species of honeyeater and about half of them are native to Australia.

Honeyeaters live on a diet of nectar, insects and a little fruit.

Yellow-tufted honeyeater

Many honeyeaters bind their nests together with spiderwebs.

Most honeyeaters have brush-tipped tongues that help extract nectar from flowers.

New Holland honeyeater

The black-headed honeyeater is only found in Tasmania.

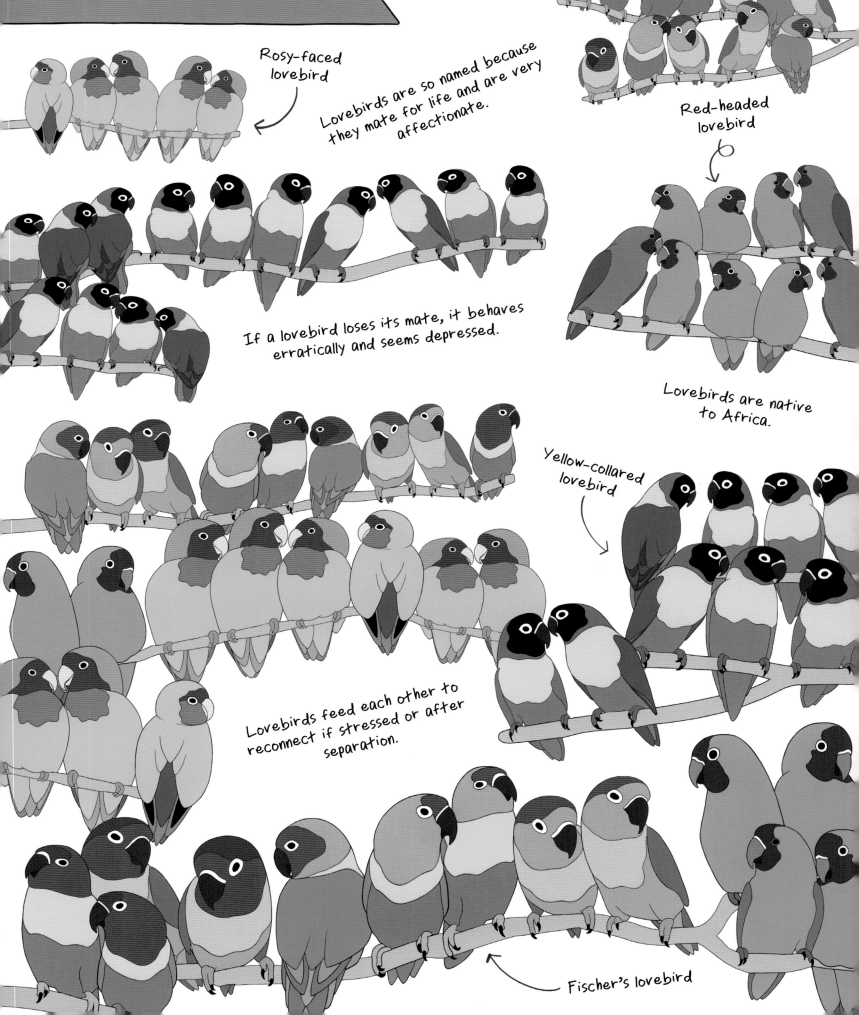

82 Lovebirds

Rosy-faced lovebird

Lovebirds are so named because they mate for life and are very affectionate.

Red-headed lovebird

If a lovebird loses its mate, it behaves erratically and seems depressed.

Lovebirds are native to Africa.

Yellow-collared lovebird

Lovebirds feed each other to reconnect if stressed or after separation.

Fischer's lovebird

Willie wagtails are usually seen alone or in pairs, occasionally forming a flock.

One of Australia's most beloved birds, willie wagtails are also found in New Guinea, the Soloman Islands and in eastern Indonesia.

Willie wagtails are named for their tails, which are constantly moving from side to side.

Willie wagtails will aggressively defend their territory from much bigger animals.

Willie wagtails are on average about 20 centimetres long, including their tails.

84 Robins

There are about 16 species of robin in Australia.

Scarlet robin

Flame robin

Australian robins hunt their prey by perching on a branch, then pouncing on the insect below.

Robins are insectivorous.

Pink robins are quieter than
most other robin species.

Robins are monogamous and share
parenting duties.

Eastern yellow
robin

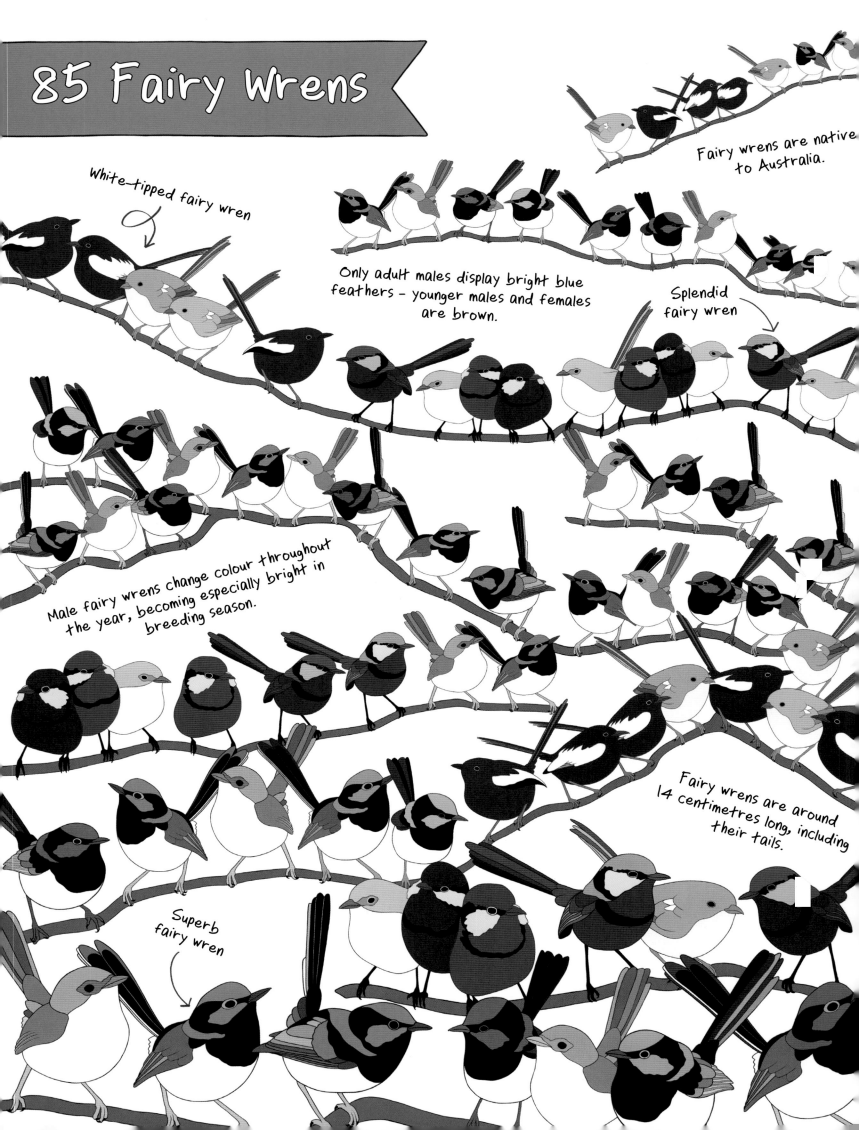

Fairy wrens are native to Australia.

White-tipped fairy wren

Only adult males display bright blue feathers – younger males and females are brown.

Splendid fairy wren

Male fairy wrens change colour throughout the year, becoming especially bright in breeding season.

Fairy wrens are around 14 centimetres long, including their tails.

Superb fairy wren

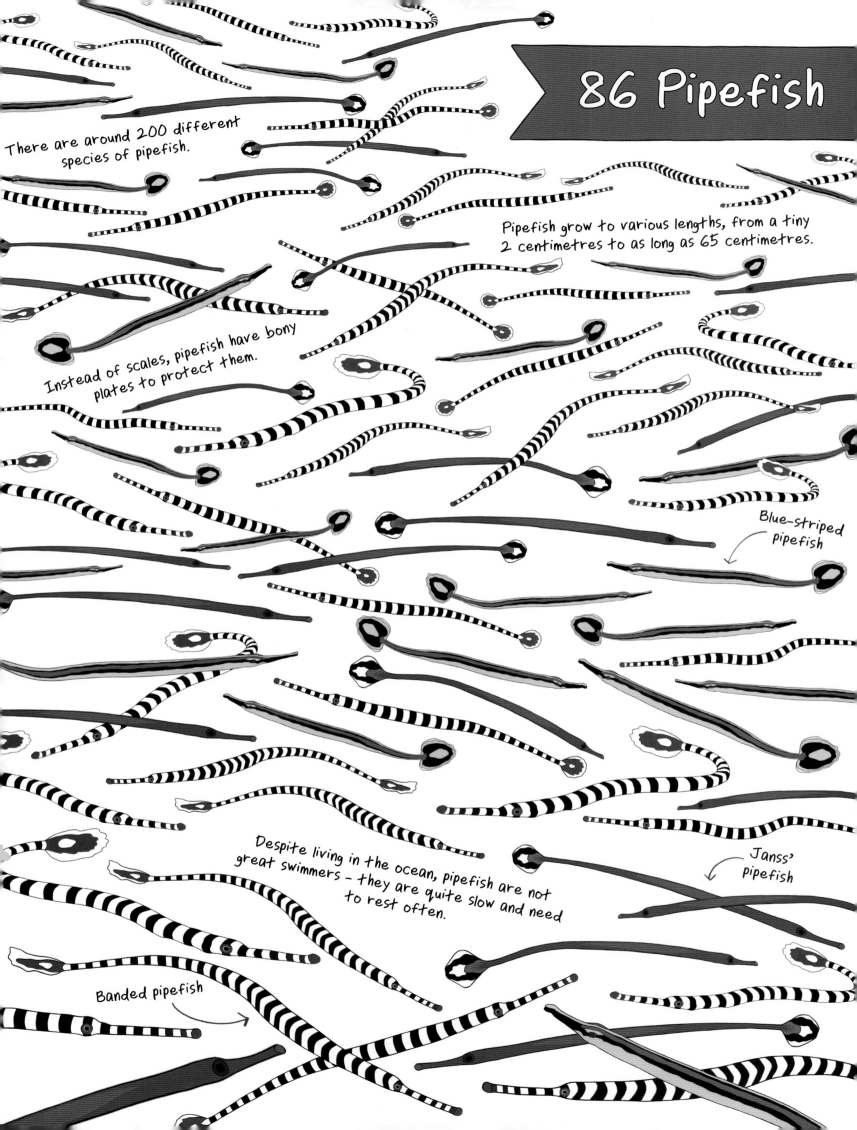

There are around 200 different species of pipefish.

Pipefish grow to various lengths, from a tiny 2 centimetres to as long as 65 centimetres.

Instead of scales, pipefish have bony plates to protect them.

Blue-striped pipefish

Despite living in the ocean, pipefish are not great swimmers – they are quite slow and need to rest often.

Janss' pipefish

Banded pipefish

87 Silvereyes

Silvereyes are native to Australia, New Zealand and the South Pacific.

Silvereyes are about 12 centimetres long and only weigh around 10 grams.

The silvereye is sometimes called the white-eye or wax-eye.

Silvereyes eat nectar, fruit and insects.

Silvereyes have amazing stamina for such small birds, with some migrating over 1500 kilometres.

Handfish are unusual because they walk on the ocean floor instead of swimming.

Handfish get their name from their pectoral fins that look like hands.

Red handfish are either red all over or with just some red features.

Both the spotted and red handfish are extremely rare and only found in Tasmania.

Each spotted handfish has a unique pattern of spots.

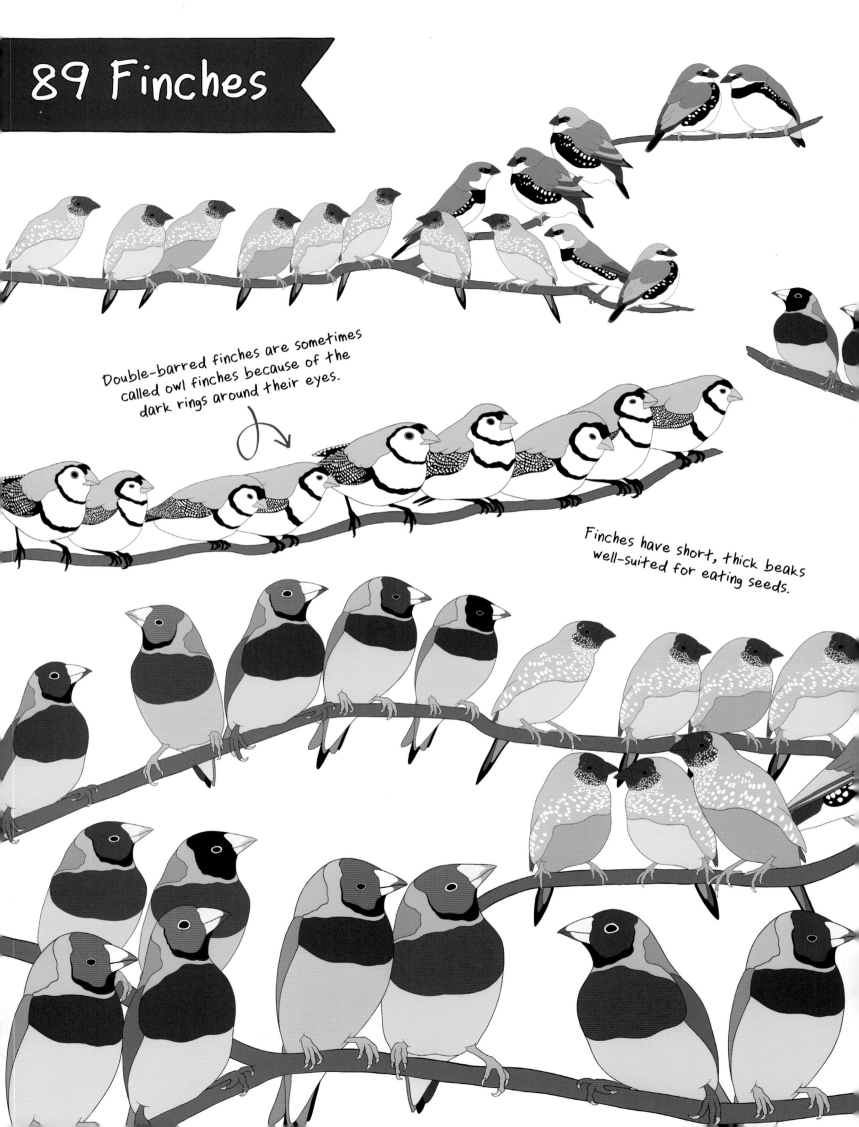

Double-barred finches are sometimes called owl finches because of the dark rings around their eyes.

Finches have short, thick beaks well-suited for eating seeds.

There are several hundred different species of finch worldwide.

Both male and female star finches perform elaborate mating rituals.

Diamond firetail finches build larger nests than most finches, with a tunnel leading into the main chamber.

There are three colour variations of Gouldian finches – red, orange and black.

90 Bee Hummingbirds

Bee hummingbirds are only found in Cuba.

The bee hummingbird is the smallest bird in the world at about 5 centimetres long. It weighs only 1 or 2 grams.

Unlike most birds, bee hummingbirds can fly backwards and upside down.

Bee hummingbirds beat their wings around 80 times a second.

A male bee hummingbird's colouring changes dramatically throughout the year.

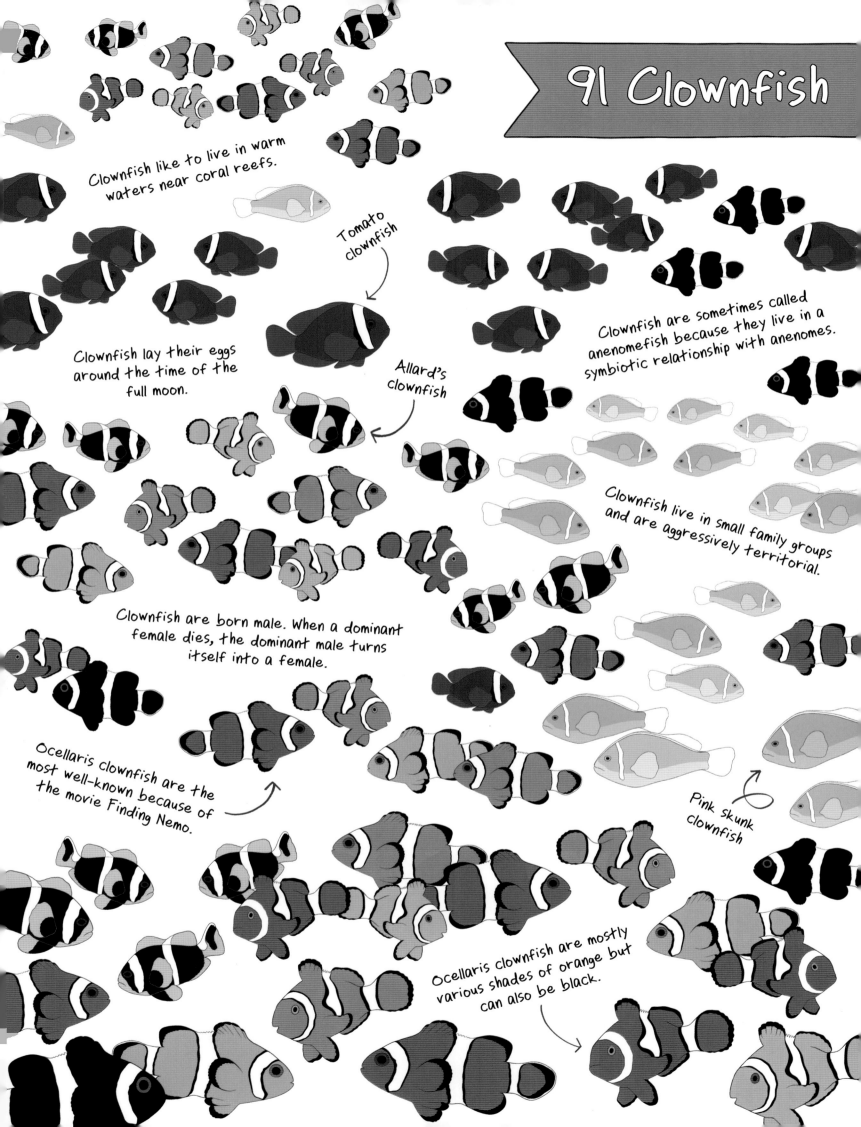

Clownfish like to live in warm waters near coral reefs.

Tomato clownfish

Clownfish lay their eggs around the time of the full moon.

Allard's clownfish

Clownfish are sometimes called anenomefish because they live in a symbiotic relationship with anenomes.

Clownfish live in small family groups and are aggressively territorial.

Clownfish are born male. When a dominant female dies, the dominant male turns itself into a female.

Ocellaris clownfish are the most well-known because of the movie Finding Nemo.

Pink skunk clownfish

Ocellaris clownfish are mostly various shades of orange but can also be black.

Butterflies taste with their feet.

The lifecycle of a butterfly has 4 stages - egg, caterpillar, chrysalis then butterfly.

Purple emperor butterfly

Red lacewing butterfly

Monarch butterfly

There are around 17000 different species of butterfly in the world.

Most butterflies only live for a few weeks.

Butterflies can't fly if they get too cold and will shiver or lie in the sun to warm up.

The Cairns birdwing butterfly is the largest native butterfly in Australia.

Tiger swallowtail butterfly

The blue morpho butterfly is one of the largest in the world with a wingspan of up to 20 centimetres.

There are around 160 000 species of moth in the world.

Elephant hawk moth

Admirabilis moth

Comet moth

Most moths have a liquid-only diet but some don't eat at all. Luna moths don't even have mouths.

Japanese luna moth

Garden tiger moth

Most moths are nocturnal while most butterflies are diurnal.

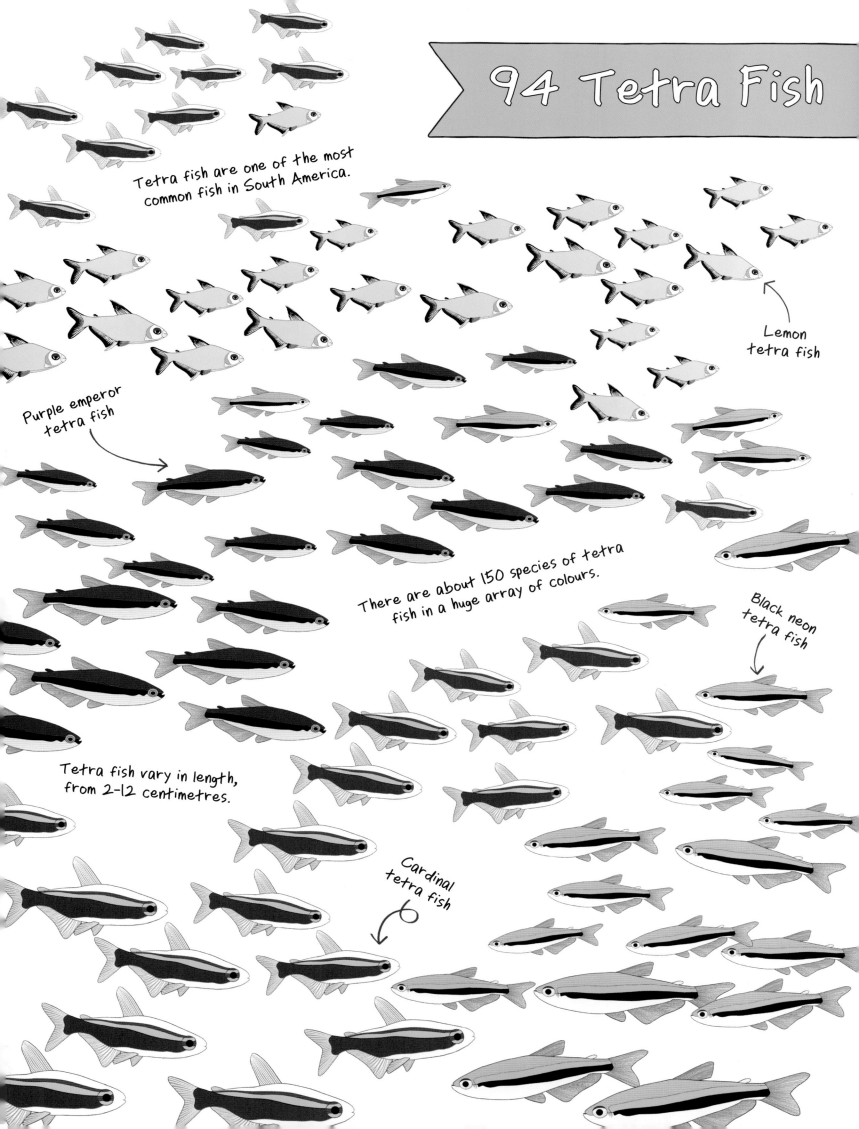

Tetra fish are one of the most common fish in South America.

Lemon tetra fish

Purple emperor tetra fish

There are about 150 species of tetra fish in a huge array of colours.

Black neon tetra fish

Tetra fish vary in length, from 2-12 centimetres.

Cardinal tetra fish

There are about 380 000 known species of beetle but more are being discovered all the time.

Beetles are found in all shapes and sizes, ranging from less than 1 millimetre in length to up to 20 centimetres.

Green fiddler beetle

Flower beetle

The devil's-bit jewel beetle is one of about 15 000 species of jewel beetle.

One out of every 4 animals on the planet is a beetle.

Beetles live everywhere, on every continent except Antarctica, both on land and in water.

Christmas beetles are so named because they are most often seen around Christmas time.

Scarlet lily beetle

The blue-banded snout weevil belongs to the sub-group of beetles called weevils.

96 Bees

Bees are important because they pollinate flowers, which allows fruit and seeds to grow.

A colony of bees consists of several thousand female worker bees, several hundred male drones and 1 queen bee.

Honeybee

Honeybees communicate by doing a dance known as the waggle dance.

Worker bees are all female and live for about 6 weeks. It takes 12 of them their whole lifetime to make 1 teaspoon of honey.

The buzz sound bees are famous for comes from their wings, which beat around 200 times per second.

Honeybees will die after stinging but most other bees can sting many times and survive.

Bumblebee

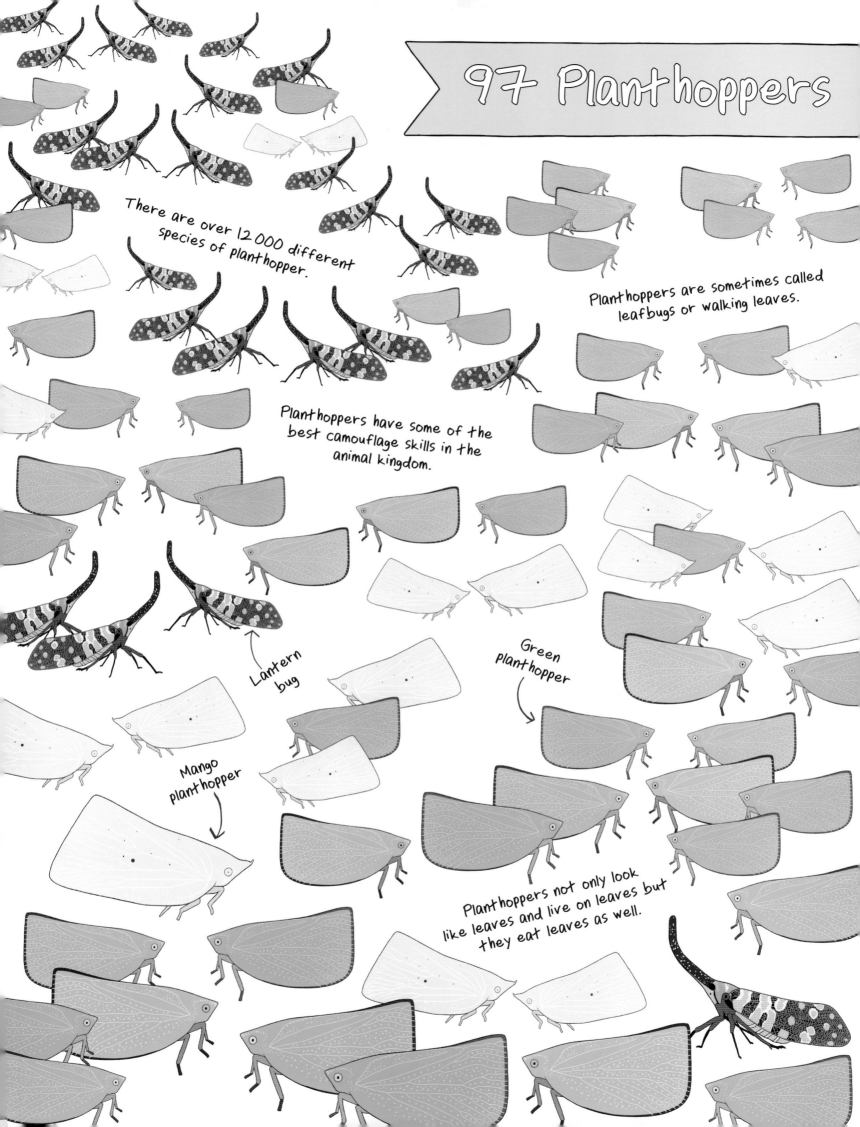

There are over 12 000 different species of planthopper.

Planthoppers are sometimes called leafbugs or walking leaves.

Planthoppers have some of the best camouflage skills in the animal kingdom.

Lantern bug

Green planthopper

Mango planthopper

Planthoppers not only look like leaves and live on leaves but they eat leaves as well.

There are about 5000 different species of ladybird in the world.

Eyed ladybird

A ladybird's top speed is 24 kilometres an hour.

Ladybirds are small beetles that grow up to 1 centimetre long.

Seven-spotted ladybird

Ladybirds eat aphids and other plant-eating pests, making them popular with farmers – they can eat 5000 aphids in their lifetime.

They are known as ladybugs in North America but ladybirds in Australia and most of the English-speaking world.

The common spotted ladybird is native to Australia and is red or orange with 23 spots.

Tortoiseshell ladybird

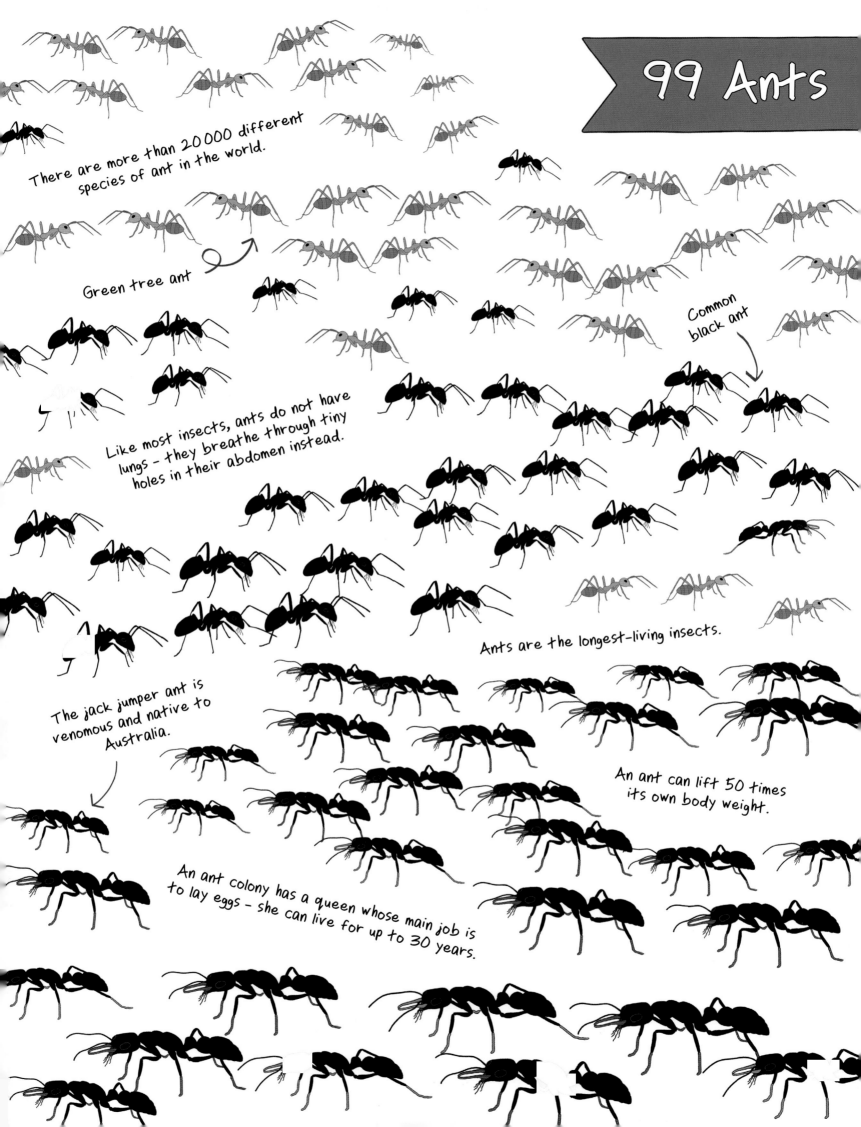

There are more than 20000 different species of ant in the world.

Green tree ant

Common black ant

Like most insects, ants do not have lungs – they breathe through tiny holes in their abdomen instead.

Ants are the longest-living insects.

The jack jumper ant is venomous and native to Australia.

An ant can lift 50 times its own body weight.

An ant colony has a queen whose main job is to lay eggs – she can live for up to 30 years.

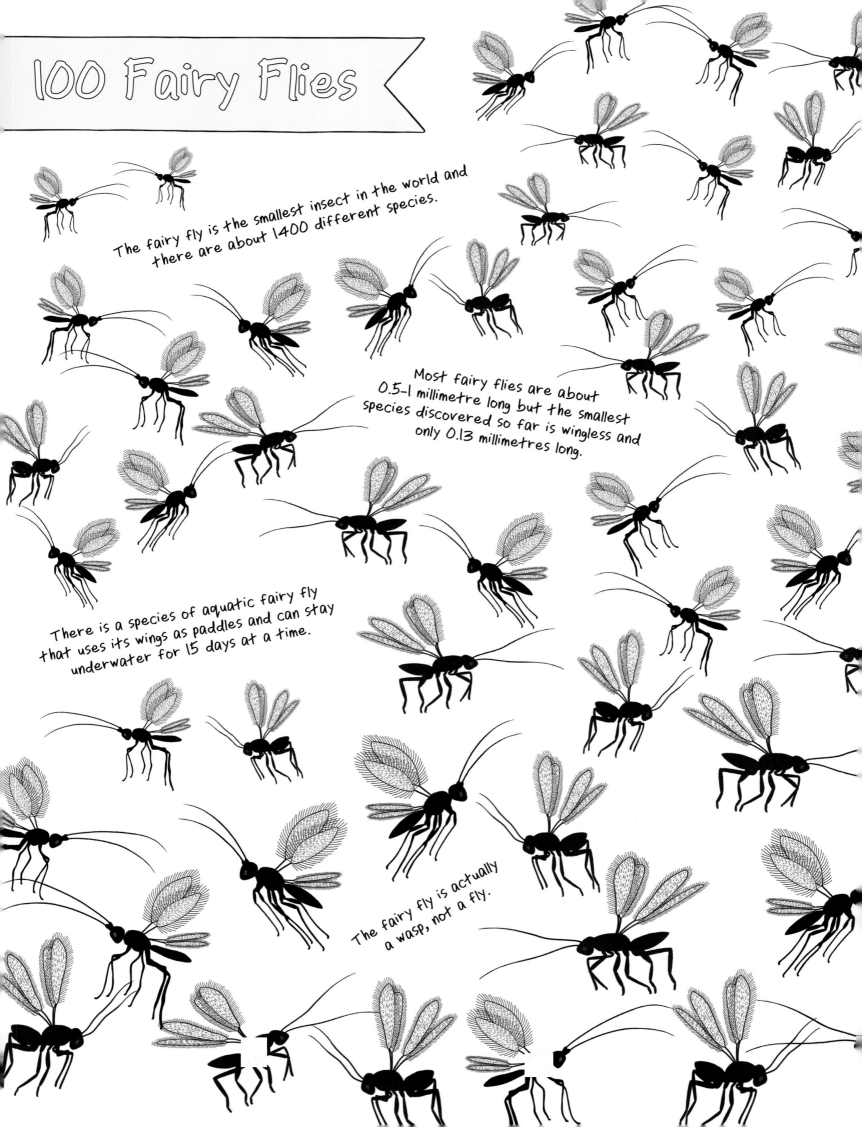

100 Fairy Flies

The fairy fly is the smallest insect in the world and there are about 1400 different species.

Most fairy flies are about 0.5–1 millimetre long but the smallest species discovered so far is wingless and only 0.13 millimetres long.

There is a species of aquatic fairy fly that uses its wings as paddles and can stay underwater for 15 days at a time.

The fairy fly is actually a wasp, not a fly.

Fairy flies eat the eggs
of other insects.

Many species of fairy fly are so small they
cannot be seen by the naked eye.

The smallest winged insect in the world
is a tiny fairy fly called kikiki huna from
Hawaii – it is 0.15 millimetres long.

Note from the author

This book was a huge undertaking. My intention was to write and illustrate a counting book that would inspire children to learn more about the natural world. Placing the animals in order of size seemed like a brilliant way to emphasise just how enormous and how tiny some creatures really are. And, of course, I do love a good list! However, I quickly discovered that ordering animals by size is not as easy as it sounds.

How do you compare an eagle with its two-metre wingspan to a wombat that is only one metre long but weighs four or five times as much? Or the tall, elegant flamingo with the short, stocky capybara? And is a cat really bigger than a chicken? Most people would say so, but there are plenty of large chickens and small cats out there to disagree!

Hence, my simple list of animals became quite complicated. I realised that an accurate list of this type is actually impossible. Should the three best zoologists in the world take up this challenge, they would almost certainly come up with three very different lists – and I am no scientist.

I have taken every measure possible to be accurate in my list and my facts, but my primary aim is to inspire, engage and entertain. If you wonder whether the rhinoceros really is larger than the hippopotamus (as I did multiple times) and decide to investigate and learn more about these amazing animals for yourself, then I will feel that my book has been a success – even if you conclude that I placed them the wrong way around!

Enjoy, question, investigate, learn and wonder. We are incredibly lucky to share this planet with so many fascinating and diverse creatures, and I hope this book will be a reminder of how beautiful and interesting the world around us truly is.

Thank you for reading,

Jennifer Cossins

Acknowledgements

This book is the biggest one I have written to date and I am so grateful for the support I've had along the way.

Massive thanks to my mum, Gail Cossins, who helped so much in researching and fact checking all the animals in this book – without her, I'd still be completely lost trying to figure out the difference between angelfish species, the way pollination really works or what on earth an unhinged jaw is! I also want to thank my nephews who were excited to chip in, with Fraser doing research for the lions page and Cameron helping out with polar bear facts. Thanks also to my sister, Jo-Maree, whose scientific brain came to the rescue of my chaotic, creative one many times, particularly when working out the best order for the animals given the challenges of being accurate with such an arbitrary list!

Thanks to my team at the Red Parka shop and warehouse, who always have my back and look after everything when I am too deep in drawing to even know what's happening in the real world. Rebecca, Katie, Lisa, Charles, Greta, Emma, Rachel and Ethan – you guys are the best!

Thanks to my Instagram family for your support, especially those of you who let me draw your cats for the cat page! I loved putting your beautiful pets in a book alongside our little cats, Tippi and Busker, who were my constant companions on this drawing journey.

As always, I'm very grateful to have the support of everyone at Lothian Children's Books, especially my editor Rebecca, whose attention to detail has made this a vastly better book.

My awesome family – I'm so lucky to have such great people around me! My mum and my sister and her family, who have supported me and my creative adventures since the very beginning. My amazing dad, whom we recently lost – we shared a great love of animals and I know he would have loved this book. His impact on me is here on every page. My mother-in-law, Sandy, my beautiful step-daughter, Tess, and most of all, my incredible wife, Tracy, to whom this book is dedicated. I'm beyond blessed that you three amazing women have adopted me as one of your own – your love, support, patience and cooking have made this book a reality and given me a chance of surviving it with my sanity intact. So, thank you for everything you do for me, for loving me and for making me happy – every single day.

About the author

Jennifer Cossins is a 2017 CBCA Honour Book-winning Tasmanian artist and writer with a passion for nature, the animal kingdom and all things bright and colourful.

A born and bred Tasmanian, Jennifer also designs homewares, textiles and stationery, which she stocks in her store, Red Parka, in Hobart.

Jennifer's other books include *101 Collective Nouns, A-Z of Endangered Animals, The Baby Animal Book* and *A-Z of Australian Animals*.

REDPARKA.COM.AU